ETHICAL DEBATES

The Debate About
Animal Testing

PATIENCE COSTER

rosen publishing's
**rosen
central**

New York

Published in 2011 by The Rosen Publishing Group Inc.
29 East 21st Street, New York, NY 10010

First Edition

Commissioning Editor: Jennifer Sanderson
Designer: Rita Storey
Picture Researcher: Kathy Lockley
Proofreader: Susie Brooks
Illustrator: Ian Thompson

Library of Congress Cataloging-in-Publication Data

Coster, Patience.
  The debate about animal testing / Patience Coster. — 1st ed.
    p. cm. — (Ethical debates)
  Includes bibliographical references (p.   ) and index.
  ISBN 978-1-4358-9648-2 (library binding)
  ISBN 978-1-4358-9654-3 (paperback)
  ISBN 978-1-4358-9665-9 (6-pack)
  1. Animal experimentation—Juvenile literature. I. Title.
  HV4915.C67 2011
  179'.4—dc22
                              2009045981

Photo Credits:
The author and publisher would like to thank the following agencies for allowing these pictures to be
reproduced: AKG Images: 12; Bettmann/Corbis: 18; Peter Brooker/Rex Features: 20; China Photos/Gett
Images: 37, 42; Stuart Clarke/Rex Features: Front cover, 39;Bob Daemmrich/Image Works/Topfoto:
Mary Evans Picture Library: 8; Najiah Feanny/Saba/ Corbis: 17; Yves Forestier/Sygma/Corbis: 26, 29; John
Greim/SPL: 45; David Hartley: Rex Features: 5; James King-Holmes/SPL: 41, 44; Makoto Iwafuji/Eurelios
SPL: 25; Karen Kasmauski/Corbis: 24; Laister/Hulton Archive/Getty Images: 28; Laski Diffusion/ Rex
Features: 10; Peter Menzel/SPL: 40; Ian Miles/ Flashpoint Photography/Alamy: 30; Ralph Morse/ Getty
Images: 19; Sam Ogden/SPL: 34; PETA: 31; Picturepoint/ Topham: 9; Jonathan Player/Rex Features: 1, 3⁵
Geoff Robinson/Rex Features: 38;Sipa/Rex Features: 6; Greg Smith/ Corbis: 16; Aly Song/Reuters/Corbis
36; Stan Wayman/Getty Images: 22; Greg Williams/Rex Features: 21;World History Archive/HIP/Topfoto:
13, 14.

Manufactured in China
CPSIA Compliance Information: Batch #WAS0102YA: For Further Information
Contact Rosen Publishing, New York, New York at 1-800-237-9932

contents

Real-Life Case Study

This real-life case study highlights some of the issues that surround the debate on animal research and testing.

case study

Animal Testing, Right or Wrong?

In February 2006, about 800 people joined a march in Oxford, United Kingdom (UK), on behalf of a new pressure group, Pro-Test. Among their number were local residents, students, and academics, all voicing support for animal testing at Oxford University's biomedical research center. The center was being built under strict security measures following demonstrations by animal rights protesters. There had also been threats from some people on the more extreme fringe of the animal liberation movement. Two years earlier, work had been suspended when the contractor allegedly retreated in the face of sustained activism by an animal rights group.

Speaking about the rally in Oxford, Laurie Pycroft, the teenage founder of Pro-Test, a UK-based group that supports scientific research, including animal testing, said: "...Students, scientists, and the public at large will not be cowed by animal rights extremists. The new biomedical research center at Oxford is nearing completion, and we must continue to speak out in support of animal research to prevent the future of medical research from being held hostage by violent extremists." Pycroft had used the Internet to mobilize support but said he had received dozens of hate e-mails, including death threats.

Robert Winston, Emeritus Professor of Fertility Studies at Imperial College, London, expressed his admiration for Pycroft's campaign. He said: "How disgraceful that a 16-year-old boy has put the medical and scientific establishment, drug companies, and universities to shame... It is time my colleagues got real. All British universities doing worthwhile research use animals, and instead of hiding, they should be boasting of their achievements." Pycroft's actions triggered a debate at the Oxford Union, which voted convincingly in favor of animal research.

Animal rights groups claim that the Oxford research center is unnecessary. They say it will be a "prison" for animals that will be treated cruelly by scientists. The Pro-Test supporters say that animal rights protesters cast scientists in an unfair light, as brutal torturers, and prevent them from speaking out about the benefit of animal research and testing. They say that a war is looming over scientific freedom and the future of progress. They insist that animal testing and research are essential for scientific inquiry and to push forward medical research and methods. These two opposing arguments are at the center of the debate concerning animal research and testing.

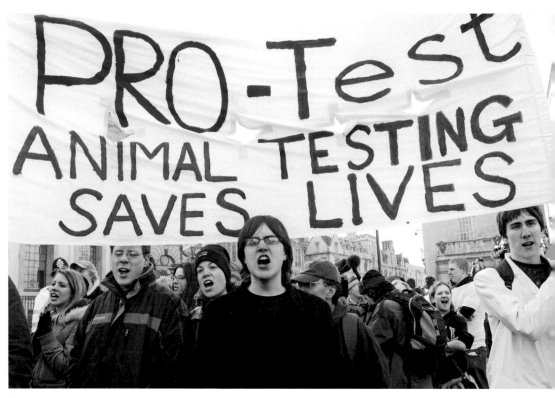

▲ Laurie Pycroft (center) and other demonstrators from the action group, Pro-Test, voice their support for animal research and testing in Oxford, UK, on February 25, 2006.

It's a Fact

Huntingdon Life Sciences (HLS) is a research organization that conducts tests using animals. In 1997, a television crew used a hidden camera to film laboratory technicians at HLS involved in acts of animal abuse, including punching and shaking a dog. When the Home Office (a UK government department) investigated the allegations, two people were prosecuted, and in order to keep their license, HLS had to put various safeguards in place to ensure there would be no repeats.

viewpoints

"I wonder whether those who object [to animal testing] to finding a higher solution for a major health problem would prefer to see a woman continue to suffer and die from breast cancer rather than accept the use of any form of animal experimentation, which appears to us essential for making any real progress in research on this disease."
K. K. Caroll, Former Director of the Center for Human Nutrition, University of Western Ontario, Canada

"Sometimes people place too much faith in people in white lab coats and assume that there's a need for animal testing just because it has been going on for so long. I believe this to be a holdover from the dark age of medical science, and more enlightened scientists nowadays believe they can get more reliable results with more modern methods."
Animal rights campaigner and former Beatle, Paul McCartney, speaks out against animal testing in 2008

CHAPTER 1

What Is Animal Research and Testing?

Animal research and testing is the use of nonhuman animals in scientific procedures. Experiments are conducted for a whole range of purposes, and many scientists argue that these experiments are of huge benefit, especially to humans. Scientists use animals to acquire knowledge about how human and animal bodies work. They also use them in medical and veterinary research, such as the development of vaccines against deadly diseases and in the testing of new drugs. Animals are involved in the development of new surgical techniques, for example, for organ transplants and open-heart surgery. Around the world, tests are conducted on animals to assess the safety of consumer products, ranging from pesticides for agriculture to cosmetics and household goods. It is estimated that tens of millions of animals are used every year in animal testing.

To Test, or Not to Test?

The word "vivisection" means the "cutting up" of a living animal. Some people use "vivisection" to describe any experiment in which live animals are involved. The use of animals in research and testing is a controversial and hotly debated subject, raising much emotion. There are many different views. For example, whether people think it is acceptable to use animals often depends on the number of animals and species used, the purpose of the experiment and its expected benefits, and the level of animal suffering that will occur.

▼ The majority of animal tests are conducted on rodents, such as mice, rats, hamsters, and gerbils. This mouse is being used in an experiment to test drugs for cancer patients.

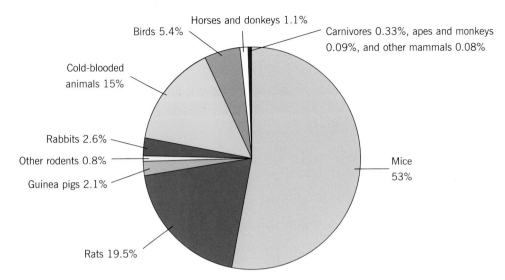

Horses and donkeys 1.1%

Birds 5.4%

Carnivores 0.33%, apes and monkeys 0.09%, and other mammals 0.08%

Cold-blooded animals 15%

Rabbits 2.6%

Other rodents 0.8%

Guinea pigs 2.1%

Mice 53%

Rats 19.5%

▲ This pie chart gives an idea of the different types of animals used in research and testing in Europe. Countries such as New Zealand, the UK, the Netherlands, and Sweden have banned testing on great apes, such as chimpanzees.

Many people hold strong, and often differing, views on whether experiments using animals are helpful, necessary, and justified. For the purposes of this book, we will refer to the people who strongly defend the use of animals as "pro-vivisectionists" and those opposed to it as "antivivisectionists."

Pro-vivisectionists point to the many life-saving discoveries that have been made with the help of animal experiments. These include blood transfusions and kidney dialysis and gene therapy for sicknesses such as cystic fibrosis and certain types of cancer.

Antivivisectionists argue that using animals in experiments is cruel and causes them unnecessary suffering. They say that animals have as much right to be treated with respect and kindness as humans. They also suggest that the results from animal experiments can be misleading because an animal's response to a drug, for example, is often very different from a human's. Many antivivisectionists insist that modern science already offers humane alternatives to animal research and testing, including the use of computer models and human tissue cultures.

viewpoints

"Without the developments that depended on animal research [during the twentieth century], our medical system would differ little from that of the late-Victorian period."
Medical research scientist, Mark Matfield, 2002

"While there are scientific, financial, and regulatory obstacles to replacing animal testing, a comprehensive review of the history of technical and policy developments suggests that there will come a time when animals no longer are used in harmful testing of any kind."
From *An Overview of Animal Testing Issues* by Martin Stephens, Vice President for Animal Research Issues and Andrew Rowan, Senior Vice President for Research, Education, and International Issues at the Humane Society of the United States

From Mice to Monkeys

The animals used in testing today include rats, mice, rabbits, guinea pigs, hamsters, gerbils, cats, dogs, birds, amphibians, and fish. Although monkeys, such as marmosets and macaques, are used in many European countries including the UK, France, and Germany, the use of other nonhuman primates, such as chimpanzees and gorillas, is now banned in Austria, Sweden, and the Netherlands. The United States is the only country that still uses chimpanzees in any great number. Rats and mice make up about 90 percent of the total number of animals used. In the UK, nearly all of the animals involved in research and testing must be specially bred by establishments that hold licenses administered by the Home Office. In the UK, it is also illegal to perform research on stray or unwanted pets (and there is no evidence of this happening). Scientists state that different animals offer different advantages—for instance, it is said that mice make good subjects for testing inherited human diseases because they share most of their genes with humans. Most laboratory animals are euthanized (killed humanely) so that their body tissues can be further examined, to relieve their suffering, or because they are no longer required as the experiment has come to an end.

Animals and Ethics

Throughout history, people have tended to believe that the suffering of nonhuman animals is far less important than human suffering. This belief has been bolstered

▼ This artist's impression of the Garden of Eden shows Adam and Eve living in harmony with the animals of the Earth.

by religion, for example, by the teaching of the Christian Church, which says that God created man in His own image and created animals to serve man.

In the 1800s, a group of scientists (most famously, the English naturalist, Charles Darwin, began to challenge this idea. As a result of his studies into the evolution of different species, Darwin developed a theory suggesting that humans were not divinely created but were simply a form of animal, living and adapting alongside all the other animals. If Darwin's theory is correct, how then do humans view themselves as different from other animals? Do humans have a responsibility to ensure that other animals are treated humanely and with respect?

The Rise of Animal Welfare

The British physiologist Marshall Hall was a contemporary of Darwin's. At his London clinic, Hall experimented extensively on animals, including newts, in his efforts to explain the reflex action. In 1831, possibly as a response to criticism of his scientific methods, Hall put forward five principles to allow for the care of animals in experiments. First, animals should not be used if the results could be obtained by another method. Second, experiments should be designed in such a way as to make the best use of the test subjects. Third, experiments should not be repeated unnecessarily. Fourth, scientists should minimize any suffering inflicted on the animals; and last, test results should be recorded properly to eliminate the necessity for repeated experiments. Hall's code of practice foreshadowed the principles of the Three Rs (see pages 40–42), which would become the ethical basis for laboratory animal welfare throughout the world.

▲ Charles Darwin (1809–82) shocked Victorian society with his suggestion that animals and humans shared a common ancestor.

viewpoints

"Then God said, 'Let us make man in our image, in our likeness, and let them rule over the fish of the sea and the birds of the air, over the livestock, over all the earth, and over all the creatures that move along the ground.'"
The Bible, Genesis 1:26

"Man, with all his noble qualities, with sympathy which feels for the most debased, with benevolence which extends not only to other men but to the humblest living creature, with his godlike intellect which has penetrated into the movements and constitution of the solar system—with all these exalted powers—Man still bears in his bodily frame the indelible stamp of his lowly origin."
Charles Darwin, *The Descent of Man*, 1871

Changing Attitudes

In the seventeenth century, the French philosopher René Descartes had argued that animals do not experience pain because they have no consciousness. In other words, they behave according to instinct, responding to different stimuli in a mechanical way. This view appeared to be widely held by many people.

In the late twentieth century, however, scientist-philosophers such as Peter Singer and Richard D. Ryder challenged this long-held idea. They argued that animals clearly have the capacity feel to pain and suffer in other ways, and what is more, should be granted the right to live their lives without having pain inflicted on them by humans.

In the early 1970s, Ryder used the term "speciesism" to describe discrimination against animals. He said: "To discriminate against others merely because they have a different physical appearance is very unintelligent. Such speciesism is as irrational as sexism or racism." Ryder insisted that scientific evidence supported his argument that animals experience pain. He said the same types of chemicals associated with the transmission and natural control of pain were present in the nervous systems of humans and animals alike. So why should animals not experience pain in the same way that humans do? This theory about pain and suffering became central to the animal rights movement, and to the ethical debate about animal experiments.

▼ In 2003, Russian scientists use monkeys to test the health effects of life in space. One of the major concerns about the dangers of space flight is that humans might not be able to endure long periods of weightlessness. Over the past 50 years, Russian and U.S. scientists have sent animals—mainly monkeys, chimpanzees, and dogs—into space to see if they can survive.

case study

Primate Prisoners

In 2002, Catherine Dell'Orto, a veterinary scientist at Columbia University in New York, reported that abuses to animals were taking place in the university's medical center. Dell'Orto told senior officials that she had witnessed primates, including baboons and monkeys, being subjected to scientific procedures where they were made to suffer pain. She alleged that they were left to die in their cages without any pain relief, rather than being euthanized.

One example Dell'Orto witnessed involved the testing of a drug designed to treat stroke in humans. To bring on a stroke, a scientist would anesthetize a baboon and remove its left eyeball to reach and clamp a blood vessel to its brain. Following this surgery, the baboons were seen hunched over in their cages, unable to drink, chew, or lift their heads. They were then given the drug and its effects were monitored. Another example involved tests on monkeys that had metal pipes surgically implanted in their skulls while under anesthetic. After the operation, Dell'Orto reported, the monkeys were given nothing but aspirin to relieve the pain. "What I saw at Columbia was apathy on the part of the employees, and almost purposeful neglect on the part of veterinarians," Dell'Orto said.

Following investigations, the U.S. Department of Agriculture and the Office of Laboratory Animal Welfare said that Dell'Orto had been right to draw attention to poor record keeping at the laboratories. However, the Department found no evidence that the experiments she criticized broke the law because the correct procedures had been followed. "We're all the losers if these studies don't go forward," said Dr. Harvey Colten, the medical center's Associate Dean for Research. "Our primary goal is the healing of human disease. The only way we can do that is through experimentation, and sometimes that involves animals."

It's a Fact

A study in 2008 claimed that 115 million animals were used in laboratory tests each year. The United States and Japan used the greatest number (17 million and 11 million respectively), followed by Canada, France, and Australia (all about 2.3 million).

summary

▶ Animals are used in research and testing for procedures including medical trials and product testing.

▶ Those defending animal use argue that it is vital for improving and protecting the health of humans, other animals, and the environment.

▶ Those critical of animal use say it is cruel and unnecessary, and can produce misleading results.

CHAPTER 2

The History of Animal Testing

▲ Galen used animal research to develop his theories about human anatomy. He was also a celebrated teacher and persuasive speaker, who never passed up the opportunity to publicize his work.

The first recorded experiments by humans on animals were conducted in ancient Greece. Around 500 B.C.E., the scientist-philosopher Alcmaeon of Croton conducted research into brain activity, which involved removing the eyeballs of healthy animals. The philosopher and zoologist, Aristotle (384–322 B.C.E.), and the royal physician Erasistratus (304–250 B.C.E.) both performed experiments on living animals. These experiments would have been conducted while the subjects were fully conscious and without the benefit of modern painkillers or anesthetics. However, as Erasistratus also conducted dissection and vivisection procedures on human criminals, it suggests that less value was placed on life than is the case today.

Roman Medicine

In ancient Rome, the early Christian faith had influenced the law, and as a consequence, the dissection of human corpses was illegal. The physician Galen (129–216 C.E.) therefore turned to dissecting pigs, goats, and monkeys instead. Galen believed that anatomy was the foundation of medical knowledge.

He argued that dissection improved his understanding of how the body works and helped him to practice his surgical technique. He was a powerful communicator and wrote many influential scientific studies.

These Greek and Roman doctors might have used arguments similar to those of scientists today to defend their experiments on animals. They were eager to discover what happens to the body when it becomes diseased or damaged, and they wanted to test and improve different treatments and cures. They believed, as many pro-vivisectionists do today, that animals were sufficiently similar to people for the test results to be relevant to human health. However, although Galen made important discoveries, antivivisectionists argue that many of his findings eventually proved to be inaccurate.

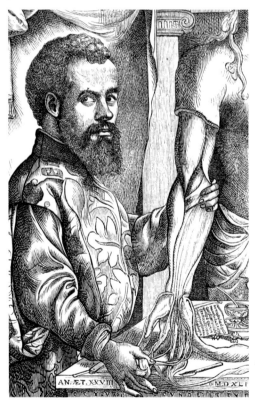

It's a Fact

In *On Anatomical Procedures*, his most important writings on anatomy, Galen described his experiments on pigs, monkeys, and dogs. He also explained that detailed dissection was essential to an understanding of anatomy, and said his inability to dissect human corpses had hindered his work.

A Lasting Theory

Galen's medical model was adopted and followed, more or less without question, for 1,500 years. The power of the Church increased, and human dissection continued to be forbidden. For a long time, humans put their faith in God rather than science, and animal experiments seemed to die out. However, in Italy, from the Renaissance onward, there was a renewed interest in animal experimentation. The dissection of human corpses was also permitted for medical research purposes, and scientists such as Mondino de'Luzzi (c. 1270–c. 1326), Andreas Vesalius (1514–64), and Gabriel Fallopius (1523–62) were involved in this work. By studying a human rather than an animal model, they made discoveries that put Galen's theories in doubt. In 1543, in *On the Fabric of the Human Body*, Vesalius wrote: "I do not think his [Galen's] ghost will be angry with me for revealing that he teaches the fabric of the ape rather than the human…" The findings and writings of these Renaissance men would become the basis of modern medicine.

◀ The Belgian physician Andreas Vesalius used human dissection to develop his theories about anatomy.

Scientific Breakthroughs

From Renaissance Italy, the revived practice of animal experimentation spread throughout the medical schools of Europe. And certainly, down the years, it seemed to produce results. Many of the most significant discoveries in physiology—including William Harvey's demonstration of blood circulation (1628), Robert Hooke's discovery of the function of the lungs (1667), and Stephen Hales's measurement of blood pressure (1733)—involved experiments on animals. But some antivivisectionists argue that blood circulation was discovered thousands of years before Harvey's time, using human dissection as a model. In 2650 B.C.E., they say, a book on Chinese medicine described the blood flowing from the heart in a continuous circle.

Moral Concerns

In the seventeenth century, concerns were raised regarding the ethics of animal testing. In 1655, the Irish physiologist Edmund O'Meara argued that "the miserable torture of vivisection places the body in an unnatural state." He asserted that, if an animal suffered pain, its distress was likely to interfere with the accuracy of the test results. Nevertheless, pro-vivisectionists argued that experiments on animals were still necessary to advance medical and biological knowledge.

◀ In 1628, an English physician, William Harvey, used a dog to demonstrate his discovery of the circulation of the blood to his peers.

The French physiologist Claude Bernard became known as the "prince of vivisectors." He believed that the relief of human suffering justified the suffering of animals. Bernard routinely practiced vivisection—even on his family's pet. In the 1880s, the French scientist Louis Pasteur demonstrated "germ theory" (the idea that germs attack the body from outside) by giving anthrax to sheep. In the 1890s, the Russian physiologist Ivan Pavlov conducted a series of investigations into the working of the nervous system by studying "conditioned reflexes" in dogs. While investigating the processes of digestion, Pavlov discovered that a dog could be made to produce saliva at the sound of a bell. This was because Pavlov had trained the dog to associate the bell with food. Pavlov later used his conditioned reflex theory to try to explain aspects of human behavior.

Animal Experiments and the Law

The nineteenth century saw the debate about the ethics of animal testing begin to gather momentum. As awareness increased of animals' capacity to experience pain, so people began to question the justification for causing animal suffering. In 1822, the first animal protection law came into force in Britain. In 1876, the British government passed the Cruelty to Animals Act, which focused on ways to regulate the use of animals in experiments. Meanwhile, in the United States, opposition to animal testing was demonstrated by the founding of the American Society for the Prevention of

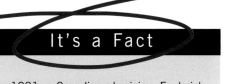

It's a Fact

In 1921, a Canadian physician, Frederick Grant Banting, and a U.S. physiologist, Charles H. Best, used the hormone insulin to treat diabetes in dogs. Their tests were successful. Regular injections of insulin were soon being used to cure diabetes in humans.

v i e w p o i n t s

"...the science of life is a superb and dazzlingly lighted hall which may be reached only by passing through a long and ghastly kitchen."
Claude Bernard, French scientist, 1865

"We sacrificed daily from one to three dogs, besides rabbits and other animals, and after four years' experience, I am of the opinion that not one of these experiments on animals was justified or necessary. The idea of the good of humanity was simply out of the question... the great aim being to keep up with, or get ahead of, one's contemporaries in science even at the price of... torture needlessly and iniquitously inflicted on the poor animals."
Dr. George Hoggan, former student of Claude Bernard and founder of the first antivivisection society in England in 1875

Cruelty to Animals during the 1860s and of the American Anti-Vivisection Society in 1883. But antivivisectionists failed in their attempts to get the U.S. government to pass animal protection laws.

Into the Modern Age

In the world of medical science, astonishing advances were accompanied by huge financial investment from governments and industries. In the late 1860s, the introduction of general anesthesia, which meant that animals could be rendered unconscious through the use of ether or chloroform, saw a huge rise in the number of animal experiments. In the UK alone, the number of tests increased from 250 in 1881 to 95,000 in 1910.

During the twentieth century, as the marketing and sale of manufactured medical drugs soared, the number of human deaths from inadequately safety-tested products began to cause concern.

In many countries, governments introduced laws to ensure that the safety of drugs was assessed before they were used to treat the general public. As a result, "toxicology" testing using animals became a routine procedure.

The twentieth century witnessed many breakthroughs in medical science. In 1922, research using dogs and rabbits helped in the discovery of insulin as a treatment for diabetes, a fatal illness. The development of antibiotics and vaccines involved much animal research: nonhuman primates, such as monkeys, were infected with polio, guinea pigs with diphtheria, rabbits with whooping cough, and mice with meningitis. As a result, millions of human lives were saved through vaccination programs. For many people, there appeared to be no argument—animal use was essential. However, others believed that causing animals to suffer was unethical, and as the twentieth century wore on, animal rights activists began to organize their ideas into a focused campaign. In a small number of cases, their activities brought them into conflict with major corporations, the scientific establishment, and governments.

◀ A researcher at a reproductive research company tests birth control treatments on a rabbit.

▲ Improved health provision and immunization against disease, using vaccines initially tested on animals, have helped to bring about a significant reduction in serious sicknesses among children.

A Vaccine Against Meningitis?

Haemophilus influenzae type B (Hib) is a form of meningitis, an illness that can cause deafness, brain damage, and in some cases, death. In 1986, a vaccination program in Finland reduced the incidence of Hib meningitis to zero by 1991. Similarly successful programs were conducted in the United States and the UK. However, the vaccine provided only a short-lived immunity to the sickness. After much experimentation, an improved vaccine was produced that showed a powerful immune response in mice and rabbits. Eventually, four effective vaccines were developed for human use. Each vaccine was tested on animals to make sure it was safe.

The Hib-meningitis vaccination program has been successful throughout the world. There has been a dramatic reduction in cases of the illness in Bangladesh, Kenya, and Chile. In Gambia, the incidence of Hib meningitis declined from 60 to zero cases per 100,000 children under five years old. Most recently, the incidence of Hib meningitis in Uganda has been reduced to zero in children under five. It is believed that the Ugandan vaccination program has prevented 5,000 child deaths a year since 2001.

summary

▶ Pro-vivisectionists say that history has demonstrated the huge benefits of using animals in research and testing.

▶ Some antivivisectionists argue that throughout history, human dissection has produced more accurate results than testing and using animals.

CHAPTER 3.

Animal Testing in Medical Research

Today, animals are used to acquire scientific knowledge, for medical and veterinary research, and to assess the safety of chemicals used in industry, agriculture, and homes. Animals are also used for educational purposes. Organizations that conduct animal experiments include academic establishments, pharmaceutical companies, chemicals companies, medical research charities, the military, and specialist commercial facilities that provide animal-testing services to industry.

The Benefits Argument

Many people argue that sometimes there is no alternative to using animals in medical research. The Royal Society (UK) says that almost every medical achievement in the twentieth century relied on the use of animals in some way. The Institute for Laboratory Animal Research (ILAR) of the U.S. National Academy of Sciences says that even sophisticated computers cannot demonstrate interactions between molecules, cells, tissues, organs, organisms, and the environment. The Institute argues that although such alternatives may be useful, researchers generally need to study a living body to see how these various parts interact and are controlled. And since there are ethical limits to the experiments they can do using people, their only alternative is to use the most suitable animal to study a particular disease or biological function.

Pro-vivisectionists also argue that, since all animals are descended from common ancestors, this means that humans share many physiological characteristics with other animals. For instance, all mammals have the same major organs—heart, lungs, kidneys, liver, and so on—that perform the same functions and are controlled by similar mechanisms. This makes some nonhuman mammals useful models for research into the prevention and treatment of a range of human diseases and sicknesses. Pro-vivisectionists insist that the wide range of medical discoveries made throughout history (and still being made today) supports this view.

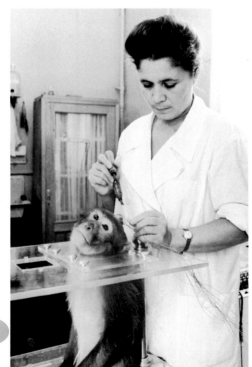

◀ A researcher in the Soviet Union in 1967 inspects electrodes that have been placed in the brain of a monkey. The electrodes give information about a medical condition that has been artificially produced in the animal.

In 1971, cancer tests were performed on goats at McGill University in Montreal, Canada. In recent years, animal rights activists have protested against the use of goats in medical and military research.

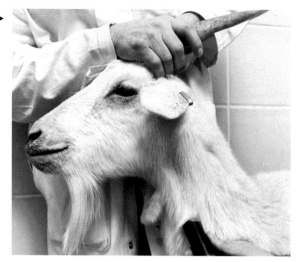

Pro-vivisectionists say that the medical advances made in the past century alone prove that animal research and testing are vital. These include open-heart surgery, vaccines against smallpox, measles, rabies, and mumps, cataract removal and hip replacement surgery, as well as treatments for spinal cord injury and stroke victims. In the 1950s, drugs developed to treat mental illnesses such as schizophrenia were tested on nonhuman primates, including chimpanzees. In the 1960s, a vaccine against rubella (German measles) was tested on monkeys. In the 1970s and 1980s, cancer treatments (including chemotherapy) were developed with the help of nonhuman primate research. Likewise, vaccines were developed for hepatitis B and HIV/AIDS, and antirejection drugs were tested for recipients of organ transplants.

Surgeons perfected their open-heart surgery and kidney transplant techniques by experimenting on dogs. More recently, scientists have developed a vaccine against bluetongue, a disease transmitted by midges that causes much suffering in animals such as cattle and sheep. As with most vaccines, the bluetongue vaccine was tested on animals. Such research has led people to ask if there is an ethical difference between causing some animals to suffer in order to develop and test a vaccine for other animals, and using animals to test a vaccine for humans. Is it justified, if the vaccine prevents animal disease and suffering?

It's a Fact

Animals were used to develop anesthetics to prevent human pain and suffering during surgery.

viewpoints

" ...animal research must continue if we are to solve serious medical problems like cancer, heart disease, Alzheimer's disease, AIDS, cystic fibrosis, multiple sclerosis, and malaria."
From the Research Defence Society web site, 2008

"...the vast majority of the most important health advances have resulted from improvements in living conditions (in sanitation, for example) and changes in personal hygiene and lifestyle, none of which has anything to do with animal experimentation."
Tom Regan, Emeritus Professor of Philosophy at North Carolina State University, 2002

Harming Animals

Antivivisectionists say that scientists often overestimate the benefits of using animals in research and testing. Some argue that the vast majority of the most important health advances have come from people's improved living conditions, not from animal experiments. They also suggest that the animal suffering involved is often downplayed, and they allege extreme levels of cruelty inflicted upon animals. They say that experiments can involve drowning, suffocating, starving and burning, blinding animals and destroying their ability to hear, damaging their brains, severing their limbs, crushing their organs, inducing heart attacks, ulcers, paralysis, seizures, and forcing the animals to inhale tobacco smoke, drink alcohol, and ingest various drugs, such as heroin and cocaine, for studies of addiction. Given the suffering often involved and their claims that many alternatives are now available (see page 40), antivivisectionists ask: how necessary is it still to use animals today?

▼ In 2007, antivivisectionists stage a protest against animal testing at the University of California, Los Angeles, California.

Central to the antivivisectionists' argument is their insistence that research and testing on animals is not relevant to people because animals are different from people. People and animals suffer from different diseases and respond in different ways to treatment. They say that reliance on the "animal model" has resulted in hundreds of millions of human deaths. For example, although certain prescription drugs were found to be safe when tested on animals, when they were administered to humans, they proved deadly. The antivivisectionists insist that misleading results from animal tests have persisted through the centuries, from the time of Galen to the present day.

It's a Fact

In 2005, an animal welfare bill came into force in Australia. One of its aims is to reduce animal testing. Instead of testing on mice, rats, and rabbits, scientists now examine human cells grown in test tubes and computer-driven testing machines.

case study

Thalidomide

The drug thalidomide first appeared in Germany in 1957. It was marketed as a sedative with remarkably few side effects. The drug company that developed it believed that it was safe enough to be given to pregnant women to help combat morning sickness. Soon, it was being prescribed to thousands of women around the world. Toward the end of the 1950s, babies began to be born with deformities, such as flipperlike limbs. Suspecting there could be a link with thalidomide, scientists undertook further tests using animals and observed the outcome closely. Since the initial tests had been conducted on animals that were not pregnant, the results indicated no problem. Eventually, after having been given 10 times the normal dose of the drug, some monkeys gave birth to deformed offspring. Antivivisectionists say that animal testing effectively delayed the withdrawal of thalidomide until 1962, by which time, 10,000 additional children had been born with severe disabilities.

▼ In Britain in 1997, the effects of thalidomide were still being felt. This young daughter of a thalidomide victim appears to have inherited deformities from her mother.

Transplants

Organ and tissue transplants save thousands of lives every year. Much of the research into transplantation, for instance, to check whether the new organs or tissue will be rejected by the body's immune system, has been conducted using animals as test subjects.

As recently as 1950, little could be done for serious defects of the heart valves. Symptoms included breathlessness, dizziness, and fainting, and deaths from heart failure or stroke were fairly common. The possibility of using transplanted valves was explored

in dogs, rabbits, guinea pigs, and rats, and the best methods of preparation and storage were established. Although the preferred solution was to transplant valves from human corpses into human patients, it was difficult to maintain an adequate supply of these. The answer seemed to lie in transplanting valves from other species. In trials in the early 1970s, valves from pigs, sheep, calves, and goats were transplanted into dogs.

Today, medical treatments that involve the use of parts of animals are routine. They include replacement heart valves from

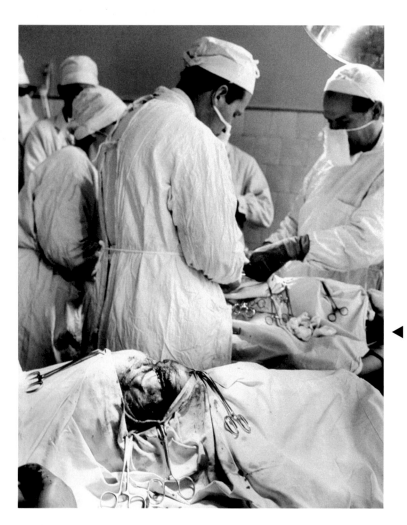

◀ In 1962, scientists transplant a heart from one dog to another. Many such procedures were undertaken to determine whether or not transplants were viable. They also helped surgeons to perfect their technique before performing transplants on humans.

pigs, and hormones, such as insulin, from cows and pigs to treat diabetes. The heart valves are processed so that they are dead tissue, and insulin is extracted from the pancreases of dead animals and the impurities are removed.

Nevertheless, thousands of people still die while waiting for a suitable organ transplant. A possible solution to this might be to use complete organs from animals, or xenotransplantation. Current research involves transplanting pig organs into nonhuman primates such as monkeys. Before they perform the transplants, scientists genetically modify the organs to try to ensure that the primates' bodies do not reject them. Xenotransplantation is a controversial practice, not least because the procedures involved can cause

significant amounts of animal suffering. The procedure is still to be successfully developed, and even if it were, many people dislike the idea of implanting animal organs into humans. However, many others argue that if xenotransplantation were made straightforward and safe, it could save many human lives.

It's a Fact

In the United States alone, between 70,000 and 80,000 heart valve replacements are performed each year, a majority of which require the use of pig valves.

case study

Extending a Life

Lucette Wells, a showroom manager, was a 78-year-old mother of three who took pleasure in simple things—her work, shopping, helping her daughter take care of her dogs, and above all, spending time with her family. However, a routine doctor's visit changed her life.

The doctors told Lucette that although her heart was in good condition, her heart valves had been destroyed through calcification as part of the aging process. The damage was such that her valves could not be repaired. The doctors recommended that Lucette's damaged valves be replaced with heart valves from a pig. Lucette's doctors told her that if they did not operate, she would be forced to give up driving,

working, and the way of life she knew and loved. For Lucette and her family, the decision was simple.

The operation went well. Within three months, Lucette was once again driving, shopping, cleaning, and helping her daughter with the dogs. She lived for several additional months. Her children say that until the day she died, Lucette was grateful to the animals that had helped to extend her life.

The organization Americans for Medical Progress (AMP) says that animal testing and research have helped scientists to improve transplant procedures. It says animals continue to be of use, specifically in the development of new anti-rejection drugs, which have fewer side effects for transplant patients.

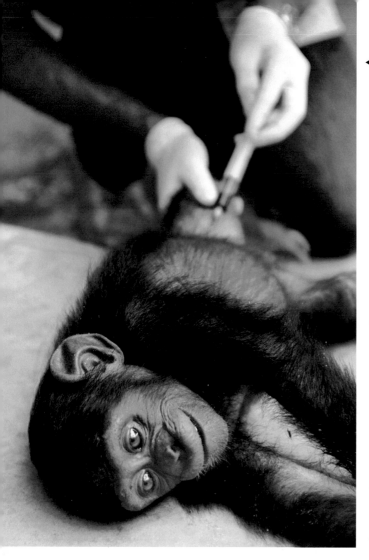

A researcher into the HIV/AIDS virus takes a blood sample from a chimpanzee.

because they had repeatedly and unsuccessfully tested it on dogs. As dogs' systems react differently from humans', the test findings were faulty when applied to the human model. Also, the antivivisectionists argue, although pigs' valves can be used in humans, they do not function as well as human or artificial valves.

Antivivisectionists say that the health risks involved in transplanting organs from animals into humans are immense, because moving an organ from one species to another involves moving large numbers of unseen microorganisms specific to the donor species. Recently, the World Health Organization (WHO) warned that proceeding with animal organ transplants could result in new diseases for humans. Dr. Jonathan Allan, a virologist at Southwest Foundation, San Antonio, Texas, said: "It only takes one [animal] transplant to start an epidemic. Only one. You are playing Russian roulette betting that a [animal] transplant won't transmit a virus."

A Vital Procedure… or Faulty Science?

As we have seen, antivivisectionists argue that an animal's response to a drug or treatment may be different from a human's. They say that clinical observation in human patients using new technologies, epidemiological research (studies of factors affecting health and sickness of population), and in vitro methods (studies of cells and tissues outside of living bodies) can often yield better information than research using animals. They point out that the development of the artificial heart valve was, in fact, delayed because scientists were unsure about its safety. This was

Vested Interests

Antivivisectionists say that there are many vested interests among people involved in animal research—from animal food salespeople to laboratory equipment manufacturers. They insist that many pointless and unnecessary experiments are conducted to boost the profits of animal laboratories, research institutes, and drugs manufacturers. For example, in spite of the millions of dollars spent on HIV/AIDS research using chimpanzees as test subjects, there is still no vaccine or cure for the disease. Antivivisectionists argue that this is because many viruses are "species-specific." In other words, unlike humans, nonhuman primates do not die of AIDS.

Despite the fact that some viruses, such as rabies, can cross species barriers, most do not. This means that vaccines always need to be developed to be species-specific. A major concern is that viruses can mutate and "jump" from one species to another, sometimes with terrifying results. Antivivisectionists argue that injecting nonhuman primates, such as chimpanzees, with human viruses could result in a lethal virus mutating and infecting billions of people.

viewpoints

"There would not be a single person alive today as a result of an organ or bone marrow transplant without animal experimentation. All the work that we did depended on the use of animals."
Joseph E. Murray, 1990 Nobel Prize winner for pioneering work on transplant rejection, 1995

"Animal models differ from their human counterparts. Conclusions drawn from animal research, when applied to human disease, are likely to delay progress, mislead, and do harm to the patient."
Moneim Fadali, cardiac surgeon

▼ In a Japanese laboratory, a rat's heart is used as part of a research program into human organ transplants.

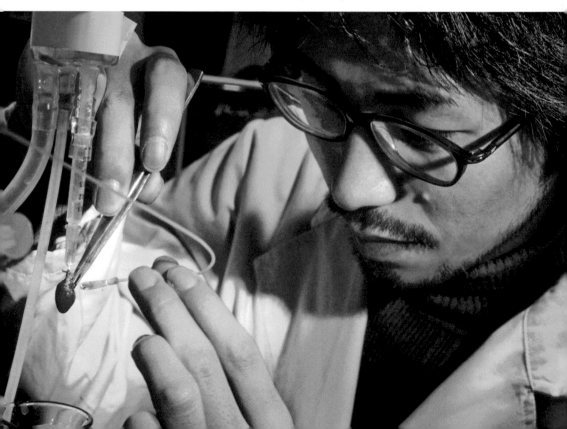

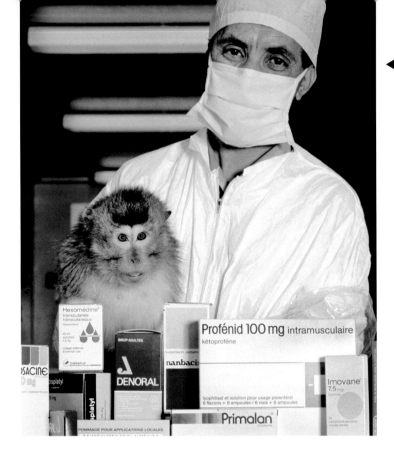

A doctor poses with a monkey alongside medicines that have been developed with the help of animal research and testing.

Medical Trials

Laws around the world demand that all new medicines must be tested on animals before they can be marketed for use by people. In the UK, safety testing of medicines on animals accounts for about one-tenth of the animals used in biomedical research. Initially, tests are conducted on isolated cells and tissues, then on animals, and finally, on humans.

Pro-vivisectionists say that this process is vitally important in protecting the human volunteers and patients taking part in clinical trials, and that a new medicine will usually be tested on more people than animals. They also say that developing a new medicine takes many years, costs millions, and that animals are used in only a small part of the process where a new compound looks as though it might have a potentially useful effect.

Antivivisectionists argue that, apart from the obvious physiological, biological, and behavioral differences between animals and humans, a further problem is that animals cannot communicate how they are feeling. They cannot say: "I have a stomachache," or "My head hurts." Therefore, unless laboratory scientists see obvious signs of sickness in their animal test subjects, they are going on guesswork and may underestimate how much the animal is suffering. Antivivisectionists say that scientists sometimes fail to predict the adverse effects of some drugs on humans. This is because these drugs have been tested successfully on animals first. Antivivisectionists also argue that animals may react badly to some drugs that turn out to be beneficial to humans. These misleading results mean that some animal tests have prevented useful drugs from being made available to people.

case study

TGN1412

On March 13, 2006, six healthy men volunteered to take part in the testing of a new drug, TGN1412, at Northwick Park Hospital in London, UK.

After being injected with small doses of the drug, the men's heads and bodies began to swell up and they became so critically ill that they had to be placed in the intensive care unit at the hospital. An observer said: "The men went down like dominoes. They began tearing their shirts off complaining of fever, then some screamed that their heads were going to explode. After that, they started fainting, vomiting, and writhing around in their beds." The worst affected man suffered heart, liver, and kidney failure, pneumonia, septicemia (blood poisoning), and had to have fingers and toes amputated.

Earlier animal tests had not shown similar responses in rats and dogs, even though they had been given up to 500 times the dosage used in the trials. The drug had also been given to nonhuman primates, in which no serious adverse reactions were observed, though the monkeys did develop swollen lymph glands at a high dosage.

Richard Ley, spokesman for the Association of the British Pharmaceutical Industry, said: "This is an absolutely exceptional occurrence. I cannot remember anything comparable." For the Institute of Science in Society, Professor Peter Saunders remarked: "Unfortunately, all species are different, and even if rodents or monkeys suffer no adverse reactions, or only at very high dosages, we still can't be sure it will be safe for humans."

summary

▶ Pro-vivisectionists say that humans share many physiological similarities with other animals, so studies using animals can provide useful information.

▶ Antivivisectionists insist that the most important health advances have come from people's improved living conditions, not from animal testing.

▶ Pro-vivisectionists say that they sometimes need to study a living body to see how its various parts interact and are controlled.

▶ Antivivisectionists say that many unnecessary experiments are conducted to boost the profits of private industry.

▶ Pro-vivisectionists state that disasters such as the TGN1412 trial would occur much more frequently were drugs not tried out on animals first.

▶ Antivivisectionists argue that the TGN1412 trial proves that animals are unsuitable test models for human drugs.

27

CHAPTER 4

Toxicity Tests

A particularly controversial area of animal use is that of safety, or toxicity, testing. An early, and crude, example of a safety test was the way in which, up until the 1960s, miners took canaries down into mines with them to warn of the danger of poisonous gases, such as methane, underground. If the canary died, the miners would know to head for the surface.

Product Testing

Today, toxicity tests are conducted by pharmaceutical and chemicals companies or by specialist animal testing facilities that undertake tests on behalf of a wide range of customers. Each year, millions of animals are used to test the dangers of drugs and chemicals to which people might be exposed. Unlike the rules

It's a Fact

The European Union is involved in funding a project called A-Cute-Tox. This aims to develop an in vitro testing strategy to replace the animal toxicity tests used today for regulatory purposes.

covering other animals used in medical research, in the United States, there are no such restrictions for mice and rats, which account for most of the animals used in product testing. The tests are conducted without the use of anesthetics, since these may interfere with the results.

◀ Miners used to carry caged birds as a safety measure against poisonous gas. Deaths from gas fumes and explosions were not uncommon down in the mines.

A dog is secured to an operating table before being used in a safety test at a health department laboratory in France.

Ethical... or Not?

Safety testing raises important issues about the ethics and humaneness of deliberately poisoning animals. For instance, is it acceptable to harm animals for the sake of marketing a new cosmetic or household product? Can the data from these animal studies be applied to humans?

Pro-vivisectionists argue that safety testing is done to guard against products that could cause damage to people, such as cancer or birth defects, or might pollute the environment and harm wildlife. They say that animal testing can provide a reliable way to gauge the effects of toxins on humans. Antivivisectionists argue that safety testing on animals is unacceptable on ethical grounds. They insist that the animals suffer unnecessarily, often for the testing of luxury or inessential products or to cover companies against legal claims for damages. They say that safety testing is outdated, time-consuming, and costly, and that alternatives should be used.

viewpoints

"The reason we use animal tests is because we have a comfort level with the process... not because it is the correct process, not because it gives us any real new information we need to make decisions..."
Melvin E. Andersen, Director of the Division of Computational Systems Biology at the Hamner Institutes for Health Sciences near Raleigh, North Carolina

"Companies are putting infinitely more money into the development of alternatives and are much more aware of... new... methods than government regulators... But the regulators say, 'You still have to prove to me that it's safe using an animal.'"
Rodger Curren, President of the Institute for In Vitro Sciences, which works with consumer products companies to develop nonanimal tests

Botox is a popular beauty treatment. But is it right that animals should suffer so that a person's wrinkles are less noticeable for a few months?

treatment to smooth people's wrinkles and frown lines. In the LD50 tests, mice are injected with samples of Botox to provide a rough idea of the potential harm to humans. The mice become paralyzed and eventually die of suffocation. As demand for the use of Botox increases, so more batches of it have to be produced and tested, which means more animals suffer. And since Botox is recognized as a medical product rather than a cosmetic one, it is allowed by law to be tested on animals.

Irritancy Testing

The Draize test is used to measure the irritancy of a new product, for example, shampoo. A test substance is applied to an animal's eyes or skin (usually a rodent species or rabbit). Some scientists have criticized the Draize test for being cruel and inaccurate, and they say it fails to reflect human exposures in the real world. A new "low volume eye test" has been developed that may reduce suffering but it has not yet replaced the original test.

An Allergic Reaction?

People's opinions are divided about the use of animals for medical research. Their attitudes tend to depend on the purpose, potential benefits, and level of animal suffering involved. However, some types of toxicity tests seem to generate a clearer response. According to the Humane Society of the United States, the majority of Americans are opposed to the use of animals for cosmetics testing. This trend is also apparent in Europe, where there has been a dramatic decline in the number of animals used in cosmetics tests in recent years. Germany, the Netherlands, the UK,

A Lethal Dose

In safety tests, chemicals are applied to animals' eyes and skin or injected into their bodies, or the animals are forced to eat or inhale the chemicals. One of the most controversial procedures is known as LD50, or Lethal Dose 50 percent. This is used to figure out how poisonous a substance is by determining the dose required to kill 50 percent of the test population. In 2005, LD50 accounted for one-third of all animal safety tests worldwide. In 2008, the *Washington Post* newspaper revealed that LD50 was being used to assess the strength of Botox, a product based on the botulinum toxin.

Although used therapeutically to treat a variety of conditions such as squint, Botox is also used cosmetically as an anti-aging and Switzerland have gone even farther and banned the testing of finished products on animals. Although legislation in the form of the European Cosmetics Directive will see a Europe-wide ban on the marketing of animal-tested products by 2013, there is currently no such ban in other countries, including the United States.

Antivivisectionists want to ensure that all toxicity testing takes account of alternative methods and other strategies limiting animal use. However, under a new European Community law known as REACH (Registration, Evaluation, Authorization, and Restriction of Chemical substances), a massive round of toxicity testing to obtain safety information on existing and new chemicals is taking place in Europe.

It's a Fact

In Canada, animal testing is not usually performed on a cosmetic product but it is used to test ingredients, particularly when new ones are developed. As a result, when cosmetics are labeled "cruelty free" or "not tested on animals," it does not necessarily mean that the ingredients were never tested on animals.

summary

▶ Pro-vivisectionists say that they are required by law to test certain products on animals.

▶ Antivivisectionists say that safety testing is cruel and can provide misleading results.

▼ A rabbit is subjected to the Draize test, which has been the target of large protests regarding its cruelty.

CHAPTER 5

The Use of Animals in Education

Animal body parts and corpses have long been used for dissection in schools and colleges. Many people value dissection as a part of science education.

The Dissection Debate

As long as dissections are conducted within the established guidelines of proper care and use of animals, as developed by the scientific and educational community, then supporters say that people should have the choice to continue with these practices. Pro-vivisectionists argue that biology teachers are the best people to judge which methods are most productive for student learning. They say that although teachers need to be sensitive to the objections of some students, there is no alternative for the actual experience of dissection.

▲ Students dissect a frog in a biology class at a school in Texas.

viewpoints

"...animal dissection enables students to develop skills of observation and comparison, a sense of stewardship, and an appreciation for the unity, interrelationships, and complexity of life."
North Carolina Science Teachers Association

"Just as we now know... that sadistic behavior toward animals in childhood is often an indicator of sadistic and murderous behavior toward humans later in life (many serial killers have a history of severe animal abuse), so also, I believe, the teaching of dissection and vivisection to teenagers is one of the most psychologically dangerous of all forms of instruction."
Richard D. Ryder, scientist and animal protection campaigner, 2002

case study

The Student Who Refused to Dissect a Frog

In 2005, Branden Skees was a student at Tidewater Community College in Virginia. He is also a vegan, which means he does not eat or drink anything that comes from animals, including meat, fish, eggs, or milk. Skees was thinking of becoming a science teacher when he left college.

However, when faced with the prospect of dissecting a frog in a biology laboratory, he refused to take part. Instead, he started gathering signatures for a petition demanding that the college provide an alternative to dissection for students who object. Eventually, he was told that he could bring his own three-dimensional animal model to dissect for his final tests. But no model was available in time and Skees failed his test.

As a volunteer for PETA (People for the Ethical Treatment of Animals), Skees had no regrets about his actions. "My father asked me if it was worth it," he said, "I replied, every bit of it. My morals and principles are worth way more to me than getting a grade."

Antivivisectionists say that there is no scientific or educational justification for dissection and that students who do dissect fare no better in examinations than students who do not. They suggest that there are many alternatives available, such as mannequins, movies, and simulators, that prove equally or more effective educational tools. They also argue that dissecting animals desensitizes and dehumanizes students and leads to a lesser respect for life. Antivivisectionists insist that education should encourage environmental stewardship and compassion for life. Dissection encourages neither, they say, because animal life is devalued and treated as expendable.

Alternatives to dissection involve using models to depict the physical appearance and complexity of animal anatomy and functions. Many of these are designed to let the student take apart and reconstruct animal structures. Another alternative is a video presentation that covers the process of dissection. Photographs and slides can also be used to explore animal anatomy and physiology. Recent technological alternatives to dissection include interactive videodiscs that allow students to do a dissection on a computer. The videodisc enables the students to focus on any layer of tissue at any step of the dissection.

summary

▶ Pro-vivisectionists say that there is no alternative to the actual experience of dissection.

▶ Antivivisectionists argue that there are many humane alternatives to dissecting animals, and that dissection desensitizes and dehumanizes students and leads to a lessening of respect for life.

CHAPTER 6

Controls, Rights, and Welfare

◀ Laboratory monkeys are happier living in social groups, as they do in the wild.

Most animal researchers today would argue that good animal welfare and good animal science are very closely linked. It therefore makes sense to ensure that animal suffering is avoided as much as possible. This should be done by closely observing animals and knowing how to recognize, assess, and alleviate or minimize any pain, suffering, or distress. Pro-vivisectionists argue that if the public understood how animal experiments were controlled, they would have more support for the use of animals in research and testing. For example, they say that the last 20 years have seen a steady trend toward improving the environments of laboratory animals. Research has shown that animals deprived of stimulation (particularly social stimulation) experience significant stress and show behavioral abnormalities. Monkeys used to be kept alone in rows of tiered cages, with 20 or so cages to a room. Although this is still the case in some countries, many laboratories now keep monkeys in social groups, with ropes and branches to climb on and with other forms of environmental enrichment.

Legislation

In many European countries, the welfare of animals in research is covered by national and international legislation, by local laws, or by ethics committees. The first country to introduce a law regulating the use of animals in experiments was the UK, in 1876, with the Cruelty to Animals Act. In 1986, the Animals (Scientific Procedures) Act introduced more effective legislation, stating that animal procedures must take place in research institutes or companies with appropriate animal accommodation and veterinary facilities.

These establishments must be licensed in the form of a certificate of designation, and the animals may be used only as part of an approved program for research or testing. Furthermore, the people conducting animal experiments must have appropriate qualifications, training, skills, and experience. The UK government also requires that the "cost" in terms of harm or suffering to animals used in an experiment must be weighed against the benefits. Pro-vivisectionists argue that these controls are more than adequate to ensure animals are not used where there are alternatives, and that animals do not suffer unnecessarily.

Causing Pain

A major area of concern is the degree to which animals may suffer pain and distress in experiments. According to the U.S. Department of Agriculture, in 2006, about 670,000 animals (not including rats, mice, birds, or invertebrates) were used in tests

that inflicted only momentary pain or distress. Around 420,000 more were used in tests in which pain relief was given, and 84,000 were used in tests causing pain that was not relieved. In the UK, tests are classified at three levels in terms of the suffering caused. These are mild, moderate, and substantial, with a fourth category—unclassified—meaning that the animal was anesthetized and then killed without regaining consciousness.

It's a Fact

Pro-vivisectionists say that although people are concerned about the use of animals in research and testing, many of them do not object to having animals killed for meat and leather products. They also point out that there are hundreds of thousands of cases of alleged human cruelty against animals every year.

▼ Laboratory dogs, like their domestic equivalents, enjoy being part of a pack and playing with a range of toys.

Distress and Suffering

How much suffering is caused to laboratory animals? Do animals experience pain and distress in the same way that humans do? Questions such as these are the subject of much debate. Descartes' theory (see page 10) that animals do not experience pain persisted in some scientific communities well into the 1980s. However, today many people accept that animals are capable of experiencing a range of negative feelings such as pain, distress, fear, and boredom. The public expects regulations to ensure that scientists take all possible measures to behave in an ethical way to limit animal suffering and use animals only where it is absolutely necessary. But, for many people, this is not enough. They say that although the vast majority of people in laboratories do not abuse animals, the existing safeguards are not far-reaching enough to control the behavior of the few who do. Furthermore, they say that the very act of confining animals in laboratory housing means that they are subjected to stress and suffering even before they are used in any experiments, because they are not free to express their full range of natural behaviors.

Animal Rights and Human Wrongs?

During the 1970s and 1980s, a number of scientists and philosophers began to question people's treatment of animals, particularly the use of animals in experiments.

▼ Scientists are conducting this experiment to try to find out more about the nature of human intelligence.

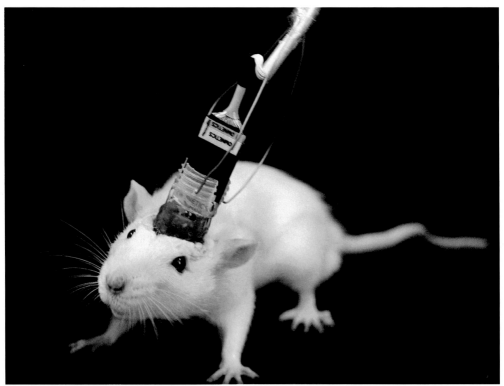

In his 1975 book, *Animal Liberation*, Peter Singer exposed the widespread abuses of animals in society. Tom Regan, an academic and president of the Culture and Animals Foundation, challenged all exploitation of animals, calling for abolition rather than reform.

So should animals have rights, even if they do not understand what "rights" are and cannot argue or fight for them? Young children do not understand what rights are either, but society acknowledges that as humans, they possess them. So why not extend this privilege to animals? Should some animals (for example, nonhuman primates) have more rights than others? Does scientific discovery of, for example, drugs to relieve human pain justify the inflicting of pain on animals? Why should the suffering of our own species be more important than the suffering of other species? Is it right to use one group of animals to help another?

viewpoints

"The question is not can they reason? Nor, can they talk? But, can they suffer?"
Jeremy Bentham, philosopher, 1789

"There is good evidence that the extent to which animals suffer and feel pain is minimal, especially when compared to our own. The suggested experience of pain in animals is an interpretation based on our own experience that we project onto the animal world."
Stuart Derbyshire, Assistant Professor in the Department of Anesthesiology, University of Pittsburgh, Pennsylvania

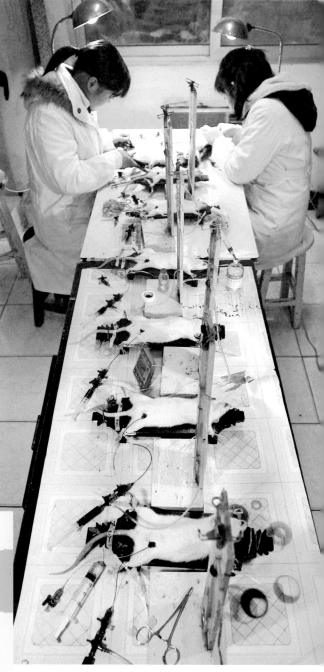

▲ In 2008, medical researchers conduct tests on rats at a laboratory in China.

Right to Life

Many antivivisectionists argue that animals have as much right to life as humans, and that deaths through research are not only unnecessary, but also morally no different from murder. Richard Ryder maintains: "One of the principal reasons why children and young people do not like science is because of its cruelty to animals in laboratories." If he is correct, then it is vital that the scientific community treats animals as humanely as possible. Otherwise, fewer young people will opt to study science and there will be a dwindling number of scientists in the future.

Animal Liberation

A curious development in the animal rights debate has been an increase in the use of violent tactics by animal rights activists. In 1999, a group of activists in the UK began a campaign to force Huntingdon Life Sciences, a research organization involved in safety testing on animals, out of business. Staff members of the company were intimidated at their homes and at work. Some employees said their cars were firebombed. In 2001, the managing director was allegedly attacked and injured by three animal rights activists wielding baseball bats.

The activists also began using more subtle methods to get their message across. By 2004, the Stop Huntingdon Animal Cruelty (Shac) campaign had persuaded eight of the company's previous clients to stop doing business with them. Greg Avery of the Shac campaign said: "Businessmen don't care about ethics; all they care about is profit. They don't make ethical decisions; they make financial ones. So we turn it into a financial decision—we will hit you where it hurts and that's hitting you in the pocket."

Scientists say their concerns about being targeted by animal rights extremists have forced them to avoid talking openly about their work, and that this has resulted in accusations of secrecy surrounding the use of animals in scientific experiments.

◀ An animal rights activist displays a poster accusing Huntingdon Life Sciences of animal cruelty in 2004.

▲ A researcher checks on laboratory rats at Huntingdon Life Sciences.

Although some would argue that animal testing in laboratories such as Huntingdon Life Sciences has important benefits, others would say that using animals in this way, for whatever reason, is never acceptable. And although some protesters claim they often have no option but to use violence to show their opposition to animal testing, many people would argue that it is always wrong to use violence, or threats of violence.

How far does the right to protest go? Should people be allowed to use extreme methods, for example, death threats, to force their views on others? Or should governments limit the rights of people to protest? Should companies expect to receive protection in order to be able to carry out authorized work involving animals? As Peter Singer remarked in 2001: "This whole area is a frontier of moral change, and there is still a long way to go before we reach consensus on the most difficult questions."

viewpoints

"... as long as millions of nonhuman animals are needlessly killed in the most grotesque forms, on the pretext of protecting human and other life, while we simultaneously allow the manufacture, sale, and release of poisons into our environment, we can never hope to achieve the goal of physical, environmental, and spiritual health we desire."
Alix Fano, *Lethal Laws: Animal Testing, Human Health and Environmental Policy*, 1997

"Animal rights activists talk about cruelty and torture, some backing their assertions by publishing out-of-date photographs of 'experiments' banned long ago. This is a misrepresentation. The work we do is performed with compassion, care, humanity, and humility."
Dr. Robert Winston, Emeritus Professor of Fertility Studies, Imperial College, London, UK

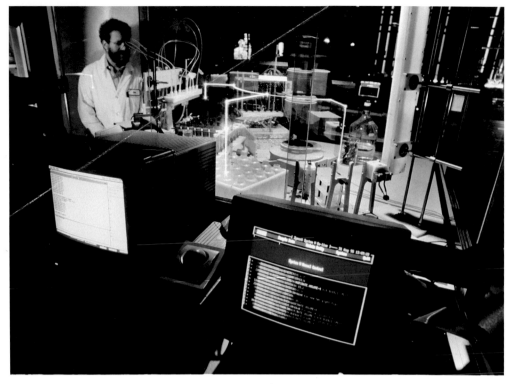

▲ The use of modern technologies, such as computer modeling and robots, can replace the need for animal testing and research.

The Three Rs

A major response to public concern about the ethics of animal experiments has been the promotion of the Three Rs concept. In 1959, two UK scientists, Bill Russell and Rex Burch, defined three principles with regard to animal research: replace, reduce, and refine. The Three Rs are now the ethical basis for the humane treatment of animals in laboratories around the world.

The idea is to replace animal testing with nonanimal methods whenever possible. For as long as animal experiments are still undertaken, scientists should reduce the number of animals used and refine the experiments and the experiences of the animals to minimize suffering, distress, or harm.

Replace

This involves research and testing methods that avoid or replace the use of animals whenever possible.

New advances in science, such as human tissue engineering, stem cell technologies, and computer modeling, mean it is now possible to replace animals in some areas of research. There have been considerable efforts to replace toxicity tests and there have been some successes, particularly in testing the effects of substances that are applied to the skin. But scientists have practical, as well as ethical, reasons for wanting to replace animal use. In many cases, it has been found that nonanimal methods are cheaper, faster, and provide more useful data than animal testing.

Reduce

The second of the Three Rs is reducing the number of animals used in research and testing. Scientists are careful to point out that numbers are reduced to the minimum necessary to achieve meaningful results. If too few animals are used, then the results will not be reliable and the experiment will need to be repeated, using more animals. If too many animals are used, the results may well be reliable but animal life will have been wasted.

It's a Fact

Researchers are trying to find alternatives to using animals in education. In 2005, Horst Spielmann, Director of the Central Office for Collecting and Assessing Alternatives to Animal Experimentation in Germany, told the media: "Using animals in teaching curricula is already superfluous. In many countries, one can become a doctor, vet, or biologist without ever having performed an experiment on an animal."

▼ A laboratory technician uses forceps to hold a tiny container of human cells. The cells are used in drug tests. Many scientists believe that better results can be obtained by testing drugs for humans on human, not animal, tissue.

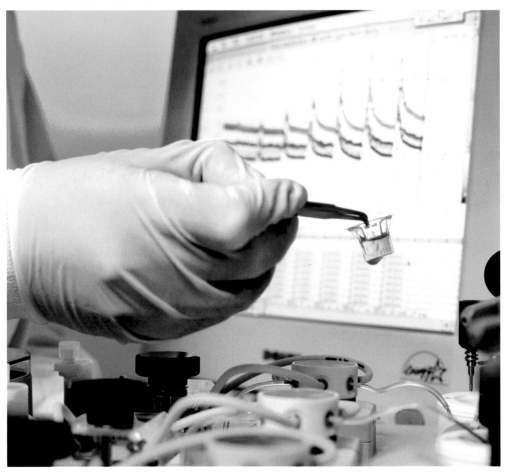

Refine

The third R, refinement, is the improvement of experimental procedures and other factors affecting animals, such as their breeding, transportation, housing, feeding, and handling. The aim of refinement is to reduce suffering and improve welfare throughout the animals' lives. Since most animals used in experiments are bred specifically for the purpose, they spend a great part of their lives not being experimented on, but living in a laboratory animal house. Refinement means adapting their living conditions so that they mimic to some extent the animals' living conditions in the wild. For this reason, animals may be kept in social groups, in large cages or floor pens, with "toys" for them to play with. Rabbits and rodents may be given nesting material; monkeys may be provided with branches and ropes to swing on and structures to hide in or climb over.

▼ The Three Rs aim to improve the treatment and living conditions of laboratory animals.

case study

In Vitro Screening System

Dr. Phil Stephens is a cell biologist at Cardiff University in Wales. He is currently developing an in vitro system to screen treatments for diabetic ulcers. He says: "Diabetes is on the increase, and as a result, 15–20 percent of diabetics will get a chronic, nonhealing wound. Some of these wounds can last for many years and they have a huge impact on the patients' quality of life. We have to get these wounds to heal. There are a number of different animal models out there, but they are not really good models for these wounds. So, we began developing an in vitro system."

The team of scientists took cells from diabetic wounds and started growing them in the laboratory. They were looking for genetic differences between normal and diseased cells. Once they found the diseased genes, they linked them to a device that activated a fluorescent light. The light switched on every time the diseased genes were "switched on" in a cell. By this method, the scientists could monitor when the diseased genes were being switched on and off, and they could target the problem cells.

Stephens says: "The in vitro system is not going to replace the animal models, but it will enable a vast number of pre-screens to be undertaken, hopefully vastly reducing the number of animal experiments that go on."

Regulation

The 2005 Nuffield Report on the Ethics of Research Involving Animals states that the UK has the most detailed legislative framework concerning research on animals in the world. However, the report adds that regulation can act as an "emotional screen" between the researcher and an animal. This means that scientists may believe that, as long as they conform to regulations, they are acting in an ethical way. The report states that researchers need to improve the culture of care in establishments licensed to use animals. Regulation is complex because animal research takes place in an international context. Many chemical and pharmaceutical products that have been developed in one country are marketed in other countries with different regulatory frameworks.

For instance, although alternatives have been internationally accepted for safety testing, there is no overall agreement on replacements for other types of research. Many tests involving animals are conducted to provide data to conform to national or international law. If one test design can be made acceptable to the authorities in many countries, this should dramatically reduce the use of animals in research.

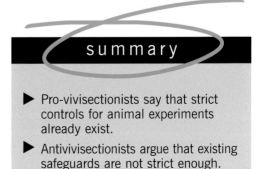

summary

▶ Pro-vivisectionists say that strict controls for animal experiments already exist.

▶ Antivivisectionists argue that existing safeguards are not strict enough.

CHAPTER 7

The Future of Animal Research and Testing

Most forms of research involving animals pose ethical dilemmas. However people decide to act, they act wrongly, either by neglecting human health and welfare or by harming animals. Pro-vivisectionists believe that despite progress in the implementation of the Three Rs, animal research remains essential. Antivivisectionists may, in principle, be able to tolerate the approach of the Three Rs, while continuing to campaign for a change in policy and putting a stop to animal testing. It appears, however, that animal use is unlikely to end completely in the immediate future.

It's a Fact

According to the Research Defence Society (RDS), a UK organization representing doctors and scientists, animal research and testing adds up to only 10 percent of all medical research.

Alternatives to Testing

There has been good progress in many areas toward developing nonanimal methods, but it is widely believed that much more needs to be done. To this end, many organizations are now working together, and governments and industry around the world are spending money to develop alternative humane methods. The greater focus on alternative methods has almost certainly been one reason for the decline in animal use in toxicity testing in the UK. However, it is not clear whether this is replicated in other countries, given the inadequacies in their reporting systems. According to the Humane Society of the United States, the situation there has been slow in comparison.

A technician tests a drug on human tissue rather than on animals. The effect of the drug is recorded, giving the scientists accurate data.

The Ongoing Debate

In 1871, Charles Darwin voiced his uncertainty about the use of animals in experiments in this way: "You ask about my opinion on vivisection. I quite agree that it is justifiable for real investigations on physiology; but not for mere damnable and detestable curiosity. It is a subject which makes me sick with horror, so I will not say another word about it, else I shall not sleep tonight."

As consumers, people expect the items they use to be safe. But how do they feel when they start thinking about the animals on which the products were tested? People fear disease and chronic sickness, so they look to scientists to relieve their anxieties about such things and to develop cures and treatments for them. If scientists say they need to experiment on animals for medical reasons, how does this make

people feel? If scientists say they observe the strictest and most humane standards, why should people think otherwise? When others suggest that animals are not good models, or that the levels of animal suffering are unjustified, where does this leave us? In the twenty-first century, the ethical debate about animal testing continues.

▲ Young people use a computer program to explore biology and anatomy in the classroom.

viewpoints

"Whenever people say, 'We mustn't be sentimental,' you can take it they are about to do something cruel. And if they add, 'We must be realistic,' they mean they are going to make money out of it."
Brigid Brophy, *Animals, Men, and Morals*

'War, nuclear annihilation, the holocaust, and the many other failures and calamities of the past century battered people's trust in science and bruised their hopes for progress. The tendency to see humans as being more brutish, and animals as more human, is understandable but profoundly wrong and deeply troubling. Such anti-human prejudice can only further erode our confidence in the human project and threatens to condemn us to further darkness and superstition in the future."
Stuart Derbyshire, Assistant Professor in the Department of Anesthesiology, University of Pittsburgh, Pennsylvania

summary

▶ Some people say there are no suitable alternatives to the use of animals in research and testing.

▶ Other people feel that there is much potential for the Three Rs to be better implemented in laboratories around the world.

Glossary

Anatomy The scientific study of the structure of the body.

Anesthetic A substance that causes loss of sensation, used in surgical operations and in dentistry.

Anthrax A highly infectious disease of animals, especially cattle and sheep.

Calcification The hardening of body tissue by deposits of calcium salts.

Chloroform A liquid used as an anesthetic during the 1800s; the patient would be made unconscious by inhaling chloroform as a gas.

Cystic fibrosis An inherited disorder that causes the lungs to become blocked with mucus.

Diabetes A disorder of the pancreas that causes excessive thirst and the production of large amounts of urine.

Dissection The cutting open and examination of a dead animal.

Ether A liquid used as an anesthetic from the 1840s to the present, though it is seldom administered for this purpose today.

Evolution A gradual change in the characteristics of a species.

Gene A length of DNA (a nucleic acid), which gives a specific characteristic to an individual.

Gene therapy The treatment of inherited disorders by replacing faulty genes with healthy genes, or by repairing or regulating faulty genes.

Hormone A substance produced by cells in the body, which has a specific effect on how the body functions.

Ingest To take food or liquid into the body.

Insulin A hormone produced by the pancreas that controls the concentration of glucose (sugar) in the blood.

Invasive Involving the introduction of surgical instruments into the body or body cavities.

Invertebrates Animals without backbones, for example, worms and fruit flies.

in vitro Latin for "in glass." A scientific procedure that takes place in a test tube, culture dish, or elsewhere outside a living organism.

Kidney dialysis A treatment for patients who have lost kidney function; a dialysis machine is used to perform part of the work of the person's kidneys.

Pancreas A gland in animals, situated near the stomach.

Philosopher A person who studies the fundamental nature of knowledge, reality, and existence.

Physiologist A person who studies physiology.

Physiology A branch of scientific study involved with the normal functions of living organisms and their parts. Physiology also describes the way in which a living organism or part of the body functions.

Renaissance An era of great scientific, artistic, and cultural revival that took place in Europe between the fourteenth and sixteenth centuries.

Stimuli Things that promote a reaction or activity.

Tissue culture The growth of small pieces of animal tissue in a sterile, controlled medium.

Toxicity The state of being toxic or poisonous; toxicity also describes the degree of strength of a poison.

Toxicology The branch of science concerned with poisons, their effects, and cures.

Toxins Poisons.

Vaccination The act of treating a person or animal with a vaccine (often by means of an injection).

Vaccine A preparation of a virus, or other type of disease, that is used as a medical treatment to give immunity to that virus or disease.

Virologist A person who studies viruses.

Timeline

1876 The Cruelty to Animals Act is passed in Britain.

1905 The first successful human transplant takes place, having been trialed on rabbits.

1910s Blood transfusion techniques are developed using dogs, guinea pigs, and rabbits.

1930s Modern anesthetics are developed using rats, rabbits, dogs, cats, and monkeys.

1940s Antibiotics that have been tested on mice are developed.

1945 The first kidney dialysis treatment is launched, having been developed using animals.

1959 William Russell and Rex Burch formulate the Three Rs.

1966 The Animal Welfare Act is passed in the United States.

1967 The first successful human heart transplant is performed, based on experience gained in transplanting organs in dogs.

1968 The UK Medicines Act rules that drugs should be tested on animals before use on humans.

1970s Chemotherapy is tested on mice.

1975 Peter Singer publishes *Animal Liberation*.

1985 The Improved Standards for Laboratory Animals Act is passed in the United States.

1986 The Animals (Scientific Procedures) Act bans the use of great apes in research in the UK; the European Convention for the Protection of Vertebrate Animals Used for Experimental and Other Procedures sets out the principles of the Three Rs; a European Union directive harmonizes legislation on the use of laboratory animals within EU states.

1992 A meningitis vaccine is launched, having been developed using mice.

2002 The Safer Medicines Campaign is founded in the UK to monitor and assess the safety of animal experiments.

2003 The European Union moves toward a total ban on cosmetics testing on animals.

2004 Australia introduces a code of practice for the care and use of animals for research.

2005 The French government contests the EU ban on cosmetics testing.

2006 The European Chemicals Regulation (REACH) details how chemicals used in the EU are to be regulated, and outlines the additional chemical testing required.

2010 New technology develops in the United States that allows cosmetics companies to test for allergic reactions without using animals.

Further Information and Web Sites

Books:

Animal Experimentation
by David M Haugen (Greenhaven Press, 2006)

Animal Testing
by Karen Judson (Benchmark Books, 2006)

Do Animals Have Rights?
by Yolanda Brooks (Arcturus Publishing, 2008)

Web Sites

Due to the changing nature of Internet links, Rosen Publishing has developed an online list of Web Sites related to the subject of this book. This site is regularly updated. Please use this link to access this list:
http://www.rosenlinks.com/eth/anim

Index

Numbers in **bold** refer to illustrations.